OF BUT

AND TREACLE TARTS:

THE HARRY POTTER COOKBOOK

A Magical Collection of Fancy Harry Potter-Inspired Recipes

Table of Contents

INTRODUCTION

Take out your wands- uhm- your ladles! A peek in this Harry Potter cookbook will help you create fancy dishes that will delightfully take you back to the pages of the bestselling books of all time.

From the food trolley favorites to the most delectable recipes served at Hogwarts feasts, this cookbook is everything about that magical world everyone in their school age and beyond would love to be in, if they had also received the Acceptance

Letter from Hogwarts School of Witchcraft and Wizardry on their 11th birthday. Don't worry, not much spell is required to help you recreate these recipes. All you need is some kitchen skills and you are good to go.

We have covered a wide range of food available from drinks to fantastic snacks, which you can pair up for a Harry Potter party, a Halloween celebration, and anything else in between. The recipes are classified into two groups: the Originals, which consist of recipes that are mentioned on the very pages of the 7-book series (butterbeer, treacle tart, cauldron cakes, anyone?) and the Adaptations, or those recipes that are inspired by a diehard fan's vision to recreate the fantasies.

This Harry Potter cookbook is for serious fans of 'The boy who lived' and his wonderful journey. If you, just like yours truly, hunger after those seemingly amazing treats that Harry and his friends got their hands into, you will surely love perusing this book. No magic required!

HARRY POTTER FAVORITES

Butterbeer

A foaming mug of Butterbeer has been featured time and again in various parts of the book as something soothing, refreshing, and comforting. Anyone would love to have it on a rainy night- or any day and any time of the day, for that matter. That's because the slightly sickly variation of butterscotch, as the author J.K. Rowling has described it, is addicting. It is definitely as amazing as you imagine it to be: fizzy and delicious! For this recipe, we intended it for minors, so the addition of alcoholic beverage was scrapped.

Refer to the second Butterbeer recipe found further into this cookbook for a kick. Enjoy!

Yield: 4 mugs

Prep Time: 30 minutes

Ingredients:

- 32 oz. cream soda
- 1 qt. vanilla or butter brickle ice cream
- ¼ cup butterscotch syrup
- Whipped cream

Instructions:

1. Put 4 16 oz. glasses in the freezer for at least 20 minutes.

2. While the glasses are chilled, place cream soda, ice cream, and butterscotch syrup into the blender, pulsing until combined.

3. Divide mixture into the frosted glasses. Top with whipped cream prior to serving.

Treacle Tart

Believe it or not, 'treacle' had been around in British cuisine long before the wizarding world was conjured in Rowling's imagination. It basically pertains to both sticky molasses and golden syrup. For the lighter treacle version, golden syrup is used in this recipe. Add lemon juice and fresh breadcrumbs, which is made from toasted crustless bread as your pastry filling and you can easily recreate Harry's favorite dessert to down all the delectable treats prepared at Hogwarts feast.

Yield: 12 slices

Prep Time: 3 hours 10 minutes

Ingredients:

For the Pastry:

- 2 ½ cups all-purpose flour
- 2 Tbsp. sugar
- 1 tsp salt
- 10 oz. butter
- 5-6 Tbsp. cold water

For the Filling:

- 1 cup golden syrup (treacle)
- 2 ½ cups fresh breadcrumbs
- Juice and zest of 1 lemon
- 1 egg combined with 1 Tbsp. water as pastry brush

Instructions:

1. Cut butter into cubes, then, place into the freezer until cold but not frozen.

2. Place 2/3 of the flour, sugar, and salt in the mixer.

3. Add cold butter cubes. Mix until the dough starts to clump. Gradually add the remaining flour and mix until your dough is broken.

4. Gently fold in 5 tablespoons of cold water until the dough comes together. Add another tablespoon if it still doesn't hold together.

5. Divide the dough into two, place each in plastic wrap, and refrigerate for at least two hours or overnight.

6. When the dough is about ready, preheat the oven to 400 degrees F.

7. Roll one of the dough in a lightly floured surface to cover the bottom of a pie dish. For the second dough disc, roll it in a floured surface and cut into long strips. These will be used as your lattice topping.

8. To start on the filling, crumble the fresh breadcrumbs in the food processor. Set aside.

9. In a small saucepan over low heat, warm the golden syrup until it becomes runny.

10. Add the syrup and the zest and juice of 1 lemon to the breadcrumbs. Mix until well combined.

11. Pour the filling onto prepared pastry dough. Lay the strips to form a lattice. Cut the edges.

12. Use the egg wash to brush the lattice and the pie edges.

13. Bake for 10 minutes until the filling puffs and the crust becomes golden brown.

Bertie Bott's Every-Flavor Beans

Not many were able to brave the challenge of duplicating the trolley favorite treat: Bertie Bott's Every-Flavor Beans. That's because they are quite difficult to make and more expensive, actually, than getting them ready from a store if you add the effort required into the equation. But if you love the book as much as we do, you will never omit any of the Harry Potter favorites available to make yourself and discover as much satisfaction as we had, especially while we are thinking up unique, out-of-this-world flavors that would impress even the likes of Fred and George.

Yield: A bowl of jellybeans

Prep Time: 3 hours or overnight

Ingredients:

- ¼ oz. gelatin powder
- ¾ cups water
- 1 ¼ cups super fine sugar
- Cooking spray
- Simple icing mixture to glue the jelly bean halves together
- Colorings and flavorings according to your preference; be imaginative, creative, and crazy!

Instructions:

1. Prepare the gelatin by adding water and sugar in a heavy saucepan. Stir gently to dissolve the crystals.

2. Bring the mixture to a soft boil until it reaches 230 degrees F.

3. While waiting for the mixture to be ready, stirring occasionally so the sugar does not crystallize, prepare the jellybean molds. Grease each liberally with cooking spray. Set aside.

4. Once the mixture reaches the required temperature, divide the mixture into different bowls, as many as the number of flavors and colors you plan to make. Whisk in the coloring and flavoring quickly so they are well combined to the mixture before it starts to set.

5. Leave to dry overnight.

6. Once ready, you may glue your jellybean halves to form a whole using an icing mixture made of sugar and a few tablespoons of water combined.

Pumpkin Pasties

One of the most delightful treats available at the food trolley that roams around Hogwarts Express is this pocket pie that is stuffed with flavorful pumpkin filling. It is one of Harry's favorites that keep his tummy stocked throughout the long train journey, something he keeps looking forward to and spending his sickles on. Why not- the flavorful combination of pureed pumpkin, mashed potato, and bacon will surely cast a spell on your palate.

Yield: 8 pasties

Prep Time: 1 hour 15 minutes

Ingredients:

- 32 oz. pie crust pastry (divided equally into 8)
- 1 lb. fresh sugar pumpkin, pureed
- 1 cup mashed potato
- 6 bacon slices, cooked and crumbled into bits
- ½ cup cheese, shredded
- 1 tsp mustard powder
- Egg wash
- Salt and pepper to taste

Instructions:

1. Preheat oven to 350 degrees F.

2. Prepare a baking sheet lined with parchment paper.

3. Whisk together mashed potato, pumpkin puree, bacon, cheese, and mustard powder in a bowl. Season with salt and pepper.

4. Roll a piece of divided dough to get a 1/8 inch thick pastry.

5. Spoon pumpkin mixture into the middle of the dough, then seal to make a pasty. Repeat with the other 7.

6. Arrange the pasties in the baking sheet, brush with egg wash, then carefully make cuts on top.

7. Bake in the oven for 50 minutes or until golden brown.

Cauldron Cakes

Another trolley treat that Harry, Ron, Hermione, and the rest loved nibbling on their way to Hogwarts are Cauldron Cakes. In the real world, they are actually similar to the devil's cake, chocolate-y and addictive, with rich glaze and mouthwatering marshmallow filling. To keep them looking authentic, you will use cupcake molds and a little bit of creativity to make cauldron feet and handle.

Yield: 12 cauldron cakes

Prep Time: 1 hour 10 minutes

Ingredients:

- 1 16 oz. pack Devil's Cake mix
- 6 oz. semi-sweet chocolate chips
- 4 Tbsp. butter
- ½ cup prepared marshmallow cream
- ½ cup vegetable shortening
- ½ cup Confectioner's sugar
- 2 Tbsp. vanilla extract
- For the cauldron handle and feet: ½ cup chocolate chips, sweetened
- For garnish: Edible gold glitter

Instructions:

1. Prepare the devil's cake mix into cupcake molds, according to package directions. Set aside.

2. To prepare the chocolate glaze, melt semi-sweet chocolate chips and butter together in a double broiler. Stirring until the mixture becomes smooth. Remove from heat. Let it sit for 5 minutes before using.

3. For the marshmallow filling, whisk together marshmallow cream, vegetable shortening, Confectioner's sugar, and vanilla extract until light and fluffy. Place it in a pastry bag.

4. Using a sharp knife or a cupcake corer, create a cone shaped cavity from your devil's cake cupcake. Dip the top part in chocolate glaze, one by one. Set aside until the glaze sets in.

5. For the cauldron feet, place the cupcake, glazed part down to three chocolate chips placed an inch from another, formed into a triangle. Press the cupcake lightly so the chocolate chips sticks.

6. For the cauldron handle, melt the remaining chocolate chips and pipe them into a wax paper, according to the handle shape that you want. Let it cool down.

7. While waiting for the handle to be ready, pipe in some marshmallow filling onto the cavity of your cupcakes. Pipe chocolate glaze around the edge of the cauldron opening. Then, garnish with edible gold glitter on top.

8. Carefully place the handle on your cauldron and you are ready to serve.

Chocolate Frogs

They may never really look appetizing but these Chocolate Frogs form part of Harry's first experiences of the wizarding world. That makes them very significant, indeed. Since, as is in the book, they are not really frogs and are instead made of tasty chocolate lumps, nothing should stop you from enjoying them.

Yield: 10-120 frogs, depending on your mold size

Prep Time: 55 minutes

Ingredients:

- 8 Tbsp. gelatin powder
- 1/3 cup milk
- ¾ cup sugar
- 2 cups cocoa powder

- 2 tsp vanilla
- Dash of salt
- 1 ½ cup milk

Instructions:

1. Whisk together gelatin powder and 1/3 cup milk. Set aside.

2. In a medium saucepan, combine 1 ½ cups milk, cocoa powder, sugar, and salt. Mix until dissolved.

3. Heat mixture over medium fire, stirring occasionally until it starts to bubble around the edges.

4. Turn off the heat before adding vanilla essence and gelatin mixture. Stir until dissolved.

5. Rest the mixture for about 5 minutes before starting to pour them onto your frog molds. Place in the freezer for 20-30 minutes until the chocolate frogs firm up.

Acid Pops

If your sweet tooth is craving for no other lollipop than those playful Acid Pops sold at Honeydukes in Hogsmeade village, you will never have to worry. You can make them quick and easy using our simple recipe featuring colorful lollies of varying flavors, sour candies, popping candies, and a bowl of honey to glue them all together!

Yield: 10-12 Acid Pops

Prep Time: 10 minutes

Ingredients:

- 1 6.6 oz. pack flavored lollipops
- 10 pcs sour candy, crushed
- 3 packs popping candy
- ½ cup honey

Instructions:

1. Place the popping candies and crushed sour candies in separate bowls. Set aside.

2. Peel off cover of each lollipop, dip lightly in honey, roll in crushed sour candies, then another dip in honey, before coating it with popping candy.

3. As popping candies lose their magic pops if exposed for long, cover your lollies in wax paper if you are not going to use them immediately.

Rock Cakes

Harry is always excited about visiting Hagrid, except for his serving of rock cakes. In this recipe, however, you will never have to elude this cookie-like, melt-in-your-mouth snack. Once you taste it, you will keep asking for more. Follow this recipe and enjoy!

Yield: 14-16 Rock cakes

Prep Time: 35 minutes

Ingredients:

- 2 cups all-purpose flour
- 1 tsp baking soda
- ½ tsp salt
- ½ cup butter, chilled

- 1/3 cup sugar
- 1/3 cup raisins
- 1 tsp vanilla
- 1 egg, lightly beaten
- 2 Tbsp. milk
- Coarse sugar to coat

Instructions:

1. Preheat oven to 400 degrees F. Then, prepare a large baking sheet lined with parchment paper. Set aside.

2. Combine flour, salt, and baking soda in a large mixing bowl. Stir in butter until the mixture gets crumbly.

3. Add sugar and raisins.

4. In a small bowl, combine egg, water, and vanilla. Pour into the dough, mixing until it comes together to form a ball.

5. Divide dough into 2-inch balls, dipping the top part on coarse sugar before arranging on the baking sheet.

6. Bake for 12-16 minutes or until the top turns light gold.

Candied Pineapple

Do you remember Professor Slughorn? That Defense Against the Dark Arts Teacher in the sixth book installment, Harry Potter and the Half-Blood Prince? Candied pineapple was his favorite. This is one of the seemingly ordinary recipes that you would find from the book and alas, it has a deep British background as a local dish.

Yield: 20 servings

Prep Time: 55 Minutes

Ingredients:

- 2 20 oz. cans sliced pineapples in heavy syrup
- 2 ½ cups plus ½ cup sugar
- ¼ cup light corn syrup

Instructions:

1. Drain the pineapples and reserve 1 ½ cups of its heavy syrup.

2. In a medium saucepan over medium heat, combine heavy syrup, 2 ½ cups sugar, and light corn syrup. Bring to a slow boil for about 4 minutes, stirring continuously until the sugar dissolves.

3. Turn the heat to low before adding pineapple slices. Turn them frequently to coat with the syrup without sticking together.

4. Keep the heat to low and simmer for 45 minutes or until the pineapples become translucent.

5. After cooking, remove the pineapples from the pan and let them dry in a wire rack overnight. You may shorten the process by baking the pineapples at 200 degrees F for 30 minutes.

6. When the pineapples cool completely, roll into granulated sugar to coat. Serve or store in an airtight container.

Homemade Toffee

Mrs. Weasley sent everyone some homemade toffee enclosed in a pack of Easter eggs at the Harry Potter and the Goblet of Fire. Apparently, it is not as difficult to recreate, nor is handling toffee for the recipe. By virtue of patience and some magical kitchen skill, you can make some for everyone to enjoy.

Yield: 3 cups bite-size English toffee

Prep Time: 40 Minutes

Ingredients:

- ¾ cup butter
- 1 cup sugar
- ½ tsp salt
- ½ tsp vanilla
- 1 cup raw almonds, whole
- ¼ cup pecans, crushed
- 1 ½ cups milk chocolate
- Cooking spray

Instructions:

1. Preheat oven to 425 degrees F.

2. Grease a baking sheet with cooking spray before laying down the almonds to roast in the oven for 10 minutes. Stir them halfway to avoid burning one side.

3. Allow the almonds to cool a little before chopping into halves or quarters.

4. Use another lightly greased baking tray to spread the chopped almonds evenly. Set aside.

5. Heat a saucepan over medium high and stir together butter, sugar, salt, and vanilla, mixing constantly with a wooden spoon until it comes to a gentle boil.

6. Reduce heat to low and continue to simmer the mixture until it is in a lighter shade of the roasted almonds.

7. Spread mixture to the chopped almonds, allowing it to cool and set completely.

8. Meanwhile, melt milk chocolate pieces in your microwave oven.

9. Pour melted chocolate onto baking the baking tray with almond and candy, then, sprinkle with crushed pecans.

10. Place the toffee to the fridge to harden before breaking it into bite-sized pieces.

Corned Beef Sandwich

Mrs. Weasley's cooking has been hailed right from the first book. Although Harry, who lived off canned soups back in Privet Drive, was pretty amazed of the mere mention of a corned beef sandwich, Ron doesn't seem so happy. For one, he doesn't like corned beef. For another, he fancies the goodies sold in the food trolley more- mostly because his family cannot afford it. That's why he was more than happy to exchange his sandwich for the goodies newfound friend Harry bought.

Yield: 4 sandwiches

Prep Time: 20 Minutes

Ingredients:

- 8 pcs sliced bread
- 1 lb. corned beef, sliced
- 8 oz. Fontina cheese
- 1 med onion, sliced
- Dijon mustard
- 4 Tbsp. butter

Instructions:

1. To assemble the sandwich, spread Dijon mustard on one side of the bread. Top with corned beef, onion slices, and cheese. Repeat with the other 3 sandwiches.

2. In a pan grill over low heat, melt butter then, grill the sandwiches, about 3 minutes each side.

3. Cut into triangles before serving.

Steak and Kidney Pie

If you think this Harry Potter cookbook is just about sweets, think again. We meant to cover everything that the book is about and more. That's why we went down to memorable Hogwarts feasts, which are always packed with extravagant dishes such as this one: the Steak and Kidney Pie. This savory and delightfully rich main course meal features beef and lamb kidneys. Both are very pleasing to the palate, especially when made into single-serving dinners.

Yield: 8-9 pies

Prep Time: 30 Minutes

Ingredients:

- 1 lb. chuck steak
- 2 lamb kidneys
- ½ cup red wine
- ½ tsp cayenne pepper
- ¼ tsp salt
- For the Dough:
- 2 ½ cups flour
- 1 cup unsalted butter, chilled
- 1/3 cup water
- 2 Tbsp. butter, melted

Instructions:

1. Preheat oven to 400 degrees F.

2. Prepare a muffin tray or mini pie pans by greasing them with a bit of oil or cooking spray.

3. To make the dough, whisk in flour and salt in your mixer. Add chilled butter cut into smaller cubes, mixing until the mixture becomes coarse.

4. Gradually add water, adjusting according to the consistency that you need for ideal pastry dough. If it becomes too dry, you will have to add more water; if it gets sticky, add more flour.

5. Roll out the dough into 1/8 inch thickness, then split in half. Use the first half for the base and the other half for the topping.

6. Cut pastry dough using a cookie cutter. Alternately, you may use the rim of a large glass. It is advisable that you cut a slightly smaller version for the top.

7. Press the base dough onto the muffin tins. For the tops, cut small slits on the center. Set aside.

8. For the filling, chop both the beef and lamb kidneys finely.

9. In a mixing bowl, add the meats, then, season with salt and cayenne pepper.

10. Scoop meat mixture onto prepared dough. Make sure that you add a bit more on the center to maintain the round shape.

11. Before sealing, pour some red wine. Place the pastry top and press the edges to seal.

12. Finish off by brushing each pie with melted butter before baking at 400 degrees F for 30 minutes.

Mashed Potatoes

Another food that is commonly served in the Potter-world is Mashed Potatoes. This simple yet savvy dish filled in for the book characters when they had too much to do or are too busy about a lot of things (which is always the case). For this recipe, garlic is added for a nice spice.

Yield: 3-4 Servings

Prep Time: 1 hour

Ingredients:

- 2 lbs. potatoes, washed peeled & quartered
- 1 head garlic
- 5 Tbsp. butter
- ¾ cup heavy cream

- Olive oil
- Salt and pepper to taste

Instructions:

1. Preheat oven to 425 degrees F.

2. Slice off the garlic head, drizzle with olive oil, cover in aluminum foil, then place on a baking tray. Cook in the oven for 30-35 minutes until the garlic is tender and very fragrant. Let it cool. Remove garlic cloves and mash.

3. Place potato quarters in a stockpot, covered in water. Season with salt and pepper, then, boil until the potatoes are fork tender.

4. Mash potatoes until it becomes a smooth texture.

5. Heat butter and cream in a pan, stirring until the butter is melted. Add mashed garlic and potatoes, mixing until well combined. Serve.

Lamb Chops

Author J.K. Rowling surely knows good food. That is evident on the food mentions he made in the book. Among them, Lamb Chops is one of the most remarkable as it is an elaborate dish that's a favorite in family gatherings and special occasions. In Harry Potter, this recipe is served in most feasts, to give students a mouthwatering treat and a nice true celebratory feel.

Yield: 4 Servings

Prep Time: 20 minutes

Ingredients:

- 2 lbs. lamb loin chops, fats trimmed
- 3 Tbsp. extra virgin olive oil
- Pinch of dried thyme
- 10 small garlic cloves, halved
- 2 Tbsp. parsley, minced
- Pinch of crushed red pepper
- 2 Tbsp. fresh lemon juice
- 3 Tbsp. water
- Salt and pepper to taste

Instructions:

1. Season lamb with salt, pepper, and thyme.

2. Heat olive oil in a large skillet over medium high until it is shimmering.

3. Add lamb chops and garlic halves, cooking until browned, about 3 minutes on each side.

4. Transfer the chops in a serving dish, leaving the garlic in the skillet.

5. Stir in water, lemon juice, parsley, and red pepper. Allow it to sizzle for a minute. Pour onto cooked lamb.

French Onion Soup

Kreacher may not be a very kind house elf, but he cooks a tasty French Onion Soup alright. He offered this dish to Harry although he knew that his master has biases on treacle tart. If you would like to know what's tasty about the soup, take a peek on the recipe below. It is surprisingly hearty, perfect for a comfort food idea. What sets it apart from the regular onion soup? Well, aside from being popular among Potter fans, it is also often served with a French baguette and used a meat-based stock.

Yield: 2 Servings

Prep Time: 30 minutes

Ingredients:

- 2 onions, sliced into thin strips
- 1 Tbsp. butter
- Pinch of salt, pepper, and sugar
- 1 Tbsp. flour
- 2 ½ cups beef stock
- ¼ cup red wine
- 1 tsp thyme
- 1 bay leaf
- Cheese croutons or French baguette in bite-sized slices, topped with Parmesan cheese and butter

Instructions:

1. Heat butter in a saucepan until melted. Sauté onions for a few minutes until translucent.

2. Season onions with salt, pepper, and sugar. Continue to cook until browned.

3. Stir in flour, beef stock, red wine, thyme, and bay leaf. Simmer for 30 minutes.

4. Serve with cheese croutons.

Roast Beef

Roast beef is a staple in British cuisine. It was also featured many times in the Harry Potter book, mostly for extravagant feasts and served with Yorkshire Pudding on the side. How can we skip the opportunity to provide you a sneak peek of how Hogwarts make students eyes roll every time a feast is underway? Here's an interesting roast beef recipe to make.

Yield: 4 Steak Servings

Prep Time: 1 hour 15 Minutes

Ingredients:

- 2 lbs. beef, top rump joint
- 1 tsp flour
- ½ tsp mustard powder
- 1 medium onion, cut into wedges

- 1 lb. carrots, halved lengthwise
- For the Gravy:
- 1 Tbsp. flour
- 1 ½ cup beef stock

Instructions:

1. Preheat oven to 400 degrees F.

2. Combine flour and mustard powder and rub onto beef.

3. Place carrots and onion wedges on a roasting tin like a bed for the beef.

4. Put the beef on top and cook for 20 minutes.

5. Reduce temperature to 325 degrees F and roast beef for another 30 minutes if you like it raw, 40 minutes if you want it medium, and about an hour if you prefer it well done.

6. Transfer roasted beef and carrots in a serving dish, setting meat drippings and onions aside. Cover the dish with aluminum foil to keep warm. You must rest the meat for 30 minutes before serving.

7. While waiting for the beef to be ready, combine the remnants of the roast beef with flour, stirring to make the lumps disappear. Slowly add beef stock until the mixture comes to a nice bubble. Season and serve with the roast beef and carrots.

Yorkshire Pudding

If there is one recipe in Potter world that seem familiar in British cuisine, it's Yorkshire Pudding. This dinner staple is a delicious filler that best goes with Roast Beef and other savory treats. You can even serve this with the Steak and Kidney Pie if you must and you will surely not regret it a bit. Once you get a bite, you will understand why, after tasting it on his first Hogwarts feast, Harry keeps looking forward to the welcome feast (aside from another school year away from the Dursleys).

Yield: 8 puddings

Prep Time: 55 Minutes

Ingredients:

- ½ lb. flour
- 2 eggs
- 1 pint cream
- ¼ tsp salt
- 2 Tbsp. bacon fat or meat drippings

Instructions:

1. Preheat oven to 425 degrees F.

2. In a mixing bowl, combine flour and salt. Create a hole in the center where you will be breaking the eggs on.

3. Gradually add cream, mixing until the ingredients are well combined. Set aside for about 30 minutes.

4. Place bacon fat or meat drippings equally on 8 muffin tins. Place in the oven and let it smoke, about 5 to 10 minutes.

5. Scoop the batter onto the muffin tins. Let it sit for a couple of minutes before putting back in the oven at a lower baking temperature, 375 degrees F.

6. Ready to serve in 15 minutes or until the Yorkshire Pudding turns a nice brown color.

Knickerbocker Glory

This treat swelling in goodness with alternating scoops of strawberry and vanilla ice cream, fresh fruits, chocolate syrup, and whipped cream is memorable not only because it is quite a temptation. In fact, everybody who roots for Harry and is annoyed with Dudley clearly remembers how a serving of Knickerbocker Glory made Harry's day during the latter's birthday when the unfinished glass was passed on to him after Dudley threw a tantrum because it did not have enough ice cream. Wonder what victory tastes like? Try this recipe.

Yield: 4 sundaes

Prep Time: 30 Minutes

Ingredients:

- 4 scoops vanilla ice cream
- 4 scoops strawberry ice cream
- 1 cup fresh strawberries, sliced
- ½ cup dry roasted cashew
- ½ cup dry roasted almonds
- Whipped cream
- For the Strawberry Compote:
- 2 ½ cups fresh strawberries, sliced
- ½ cup sugar
- ½ tsp lemon juice
- 2 Tbsp. water

Instructions:

1. Combine sliced strawberries with sugar, lemon juice, and water.

2. Transfer into a pan, then cook over low heat for about 20 minutes. Let it cool.

3. When you are ready to assemble, lay some strawberries at the edge of a tall glass. Add one scoop each of ice cream,

then, scoop strawberry compote and stir in chopped nuts. Top with whipped cream before serving. You may also add other fresh fruits, including peaches and cherries, and a drizzle of chocolate syrup for a more delectable outcome.

Exploding Bonbons

The famous sweet shop Honeydukes, located at the Hogsmeade Village, offers an assortment of treats that you could not resist. Exploding Bonbons is a favorite among humor lovers Fred and George Weasley as it gives them a good laugh every time. Sadly, it was forbidden to explode when Professor Umbridge entered the scene at Book 5.

Yield: 12 truffles

Prep Time: 3 hours 25 Minutes

Ingredients:

- 6 oz. bittersweet chocolate chips
- 4 oz. heavy cream
- 5 packets popping candy

- 12 oz. chocolate candy coating

Instructions:

1. Simmer cream in a small saucepan over medium heat.

2. Transfer hot cream to a bigger bowl with the chocolate chips, stirring until the mixture becomes smooth.

3. Cover the bowl with plastic wrap, then chill for about 3 hours.

4. Scoop chocolate ganache in an aluminum foil lined baking sheet to form ¾-inch balls.

5. Pop the baking sheet into the freezer and leave it for about 5-10 minutes while preparing the chocolate candy coating dip according to package directions.

6. Once ready, dip the popping candy coated chocolate balls on the chocolate candy coating until fully covered. Sprinkle the bonbons with more popping candies for garnish as well as an added bang!

Chocolate Gateau

There are many desserts that were mentioned in Harry Potter pages and this one somehow sticks. The mere mention of chocolate made it something wonderful to look forward to. Rowling seems to have fondness for chocolates. She used it not just as comfort food but also to ward off the ill effects of the presence of dementors. For this rich chocolate recipe, the rich triple decker cake is a sure stealer, along with the melts-in-your-mouth goodness of salted caramel and chocolate frosting.

Yield: 8-10 Servings

Prep Time: 1 hour

Ingredients:

- 1 ¼ cups flour
- 12 Tbsp. butter, softened
- ½ cup almond flour
- 1 ¼ tsp baking soda
- ½ tsp baking powder
- 1 tsp salt
- ¾ cup hot water
- 4 oz. unsweetened chocolate
- ¼ cup cocoa powder
- 1 ¾ cup sugar
- 4 eggs
- 2 egg yolks
- 2 tsp vanilla extract
- ¾ cup sour cream
- 2 cups bittersweet chocolate frosting

Instructions:

1. Preheat oven to 350 degrees F. Prepare 3 8-inch cake pans, greased with oil. Set aside.

2. Combine hot water, chocolate, and cocoa powder in a heatproof mixing bowl.

3. Place bowl in bain-marie, stirring mixture until combined.

4. Stir in sugar, mixing until smooth. Set aside.

5. Mix flour, almond flour, salt, baking soda, and baking powder.

6. Get another bowl and whisk together eggs and egg yolks. Add remaining sugar, mixing until creamy.

7. Stir in chocolate mixture until well combined.

8. Gradually fold in flour mixture, sour cream, and vanilla extract, mixing until the ingredients are well combined.

9. Divide batter onto three cake pans, spreading evenly.

10. Bake for 30 minutes or until a toothpick comes clean. Let cool in a wire rack.

11. Frost cake with bittersweet chocolate icing, placing ¼-in thick layer in between before coating the top and the sides. Use a scraper to smoothen cake until glossy.

Pumpkin Juice

A great drink to have at hand when you only want to chill and relax, a glass of pumpkin juice would never get you wrong as it did to the characters in the book. For this recipe, butternut squash is used to make the juice. Then, it is mixed with a handful of other goodies for a delectable finish.

Yield: 2 Servings

Prep Time: 10 Minutes

Ingredients:

- 1 cup butternut squash slices
- 1 red apple, cored
- 1 lemon
- 1 inch piece of ginger, skinned

Instructions:

1. Use a juicer to juice all the ingredients.

2. Discard the solids by straining the juice in a fine mesh.

3. Transfer in glasses with ice cubes.

MAGICAL MEAL IDEAS C/O A MUGGLE FAN

Boozed Butterbeer

Any fanatic would love to get a sip of this iconic beverage from Hogsmeade. It's a mystical, whimsical, and magical drink that resembles beer, with a beautiful base amber color and a creamy smooth top. For this version, we decided to stuff the booze, which means it is perfect for persons of legal age to enjoy a light kick of alcohol. Its taste may be unfamiliar to Muggles like you and me, yet we are sure to crave the taste of this soothing and smooth concoction.

Yield: 4 mugs

Prep Time: 3 hours 20 minutes

Ingredients:

- 1 L cream soda
- 1 cup heavy cream

- 1/3 cup butterscotch sauce
- 1 oz. butterscotch schnapps or Bailey's Irish cream

Instructions:

1. Pour soda into a large shallow dish. Use a 9×13 container or a mixing bowl big enough for all the ingredients.

2. Booze up your mixture a little bit by adding 1 oz. of butterscotch schnapps or Bailey's Irish cream. Place the mixture without the lid in the freezer for 30 minutes or until it starts to get frozen around the edges.

3. Remove the mixture from freezer, break up the frozen edges, and rake the frozen bits to the center with a fork. Put it back in the freezer for another 30 minutes, repeating the process until the mixture becomes slushy. This will usually take 3 hours if you start with a mixture at room temperature. But you may shorten the time with a chilled soda or a colder freezer temp.

4. When the soda mixture is almost ready, prepare the topping by beating heavy cream until it is lightened but still loose, similar to a beer foam.

5. Whisk in butterscotch sauce for that unique butterbeer flavor. Mix well.

6. Pour slushy soda into the beer mugs. Then, spoon the foamy topping on top. You may serve it with or without a straw, but gulping the concoction straight up will give you a nice mustache.

After Quidditch Dinner

Every hardcore Potter fan knows that Quidditch is a well-loved game in the wizarding world. Imagine how exhausted Quidditch players come out of the field that they seem like they could down an entire cow. To keep them inspired, which will hold them through practice and the actual game as well, here is a tweaked Shepherd's Pie recipe especially made with love. This is perfect for those days when you are tired and hungry and the best thing you would want in the world is a treat at the dinner table.

Yield: 8 slices

Prep Time: 50 minutes

Ingredients:

- 1 lb. ground beef
- 1 clove garlic, crushed
- ½ cup onion, diced
- ½ cup carrot, diced
- ½ cup frozen peas
- 2 medium jalapeno peppers, seeded
- 1 pack gravy mix, prepared according to package directions
- 2 cups mashed potatoes
- ½ cup extra sharp Cheddar cheese, shredded
- Smoked paprika
- Cooking spray

Instructions:

1. Preheat the oven to 350 degrees F. Grease a casserole dish with a cooking spray. Set aside.

2. In a large skillet, over the medium high heat, cook ground beef. Stir until it turns brown, about 5 to 7 minutes. Transfer in a bowl. Set aside.

3. Remove much of the oil from the pan. Sauté onion, garlic, carrots, and jalapenos. Stir occasionally until the veggies softened.

4. Add frozen peas and cook for another 3 minutes.

5. Stir in browned beef and prepared gravy. Mix until combined.

6. Transfer the beef mixture onto the casserole dish. Cover with a layer of mashed potatoes, then, top with cheese and a dash of paprika.

7. Bake for 15 minutes. Broil the pie further for 2 minutes until the cheese turns golden brown.

8. Rest for at least 10 minutes prior to serving.

Creamy Violet Cheesecake

We never really get to know how yummy Aunt Petunia's violet pudding was since house elf Dobby blasted it into pieces. That's why it landed on this group. Had Rowling made more vivid descriptions of the dessert before it levitated to the ceiling and crashed down on the head of Vernon Dursley's business associate's wife, Mrs. Mason, we could have made a closer version to life. For now, make do with this craft-fully made lemon cheesecake featuring a vanilla wafer crust.

Yield: 16 cheesecake slices

Prep Time: 4 hours 30 minutes

Ingredients:

- 1 ½ cups vanilla wafer, crushed into crumbs
- ¼ cup + 1 Tbsp. unsalted butter, melted
- 2 Tbsp. sugar
- 2-8 oz. package cream cheese at room temperature
- 1 cup sour cream
- 1 cup sugar
- 3 eggs
- 1 tsp vanilla extract
- 2 Tbsp. lemon juice
- Zest of 1 lemon
- Violet flowers
- Confectioner's sugar
- 1 Egg white

Instructions:

1. Preheat oven to 325 degrees F.

2. Use 1 Tbsp. butter to grease the base of an 8-inch springform pan. Cover the bottom of the pan with several layers of aluminum foil to make sure liquid will not creep through during the baking process.

3. In a mixing bowl, combine crushed vanilla wafers, melted butter, and 2 Tbsp. sugar. Stir until the mixture looks like wet sand.

4. Press the crumbs onto the bottom of the pan. Set aside.

5. Cream together cream cheeses and sugar in a mixer.

6. Stir in sour cream, vanilla, lemon zest and juice. Process at high speed until the ingredients are incorporated.

7. Gradually add eggs, one at a time, then, fully blend into a smooth filling.

8. Transfer the filling onto prepared crust. Then, place the cheesecake in a roasting pan with boiling water filling halfway up. Bake for 50 minutes.

9. After 50 minutes, turn off the oven but leave the cheesecake with the door closed for another 1 hour.

10. Remove the cheesecake from the pan and place it in a cooling rack until it settles completely, about 1 to 2 hours.

11. For the sugared violets, coat the violet flowers with egg white before dusting them off with fine Confectioner's sugar. Use them to garnish your cheesecake.

Spiced Dragon Roasted Nuts

The concept for dragon roasted chestnuts was mentioned on the sixth installment of the Harry Potter movies but it was not anywhere in the book version of the Half-Blood Prince. That does not make it worthless for this recipe book, however, as it proves to be very interesting, especially with the spicy kick and the idea that it was inspired by Charlie Weasley's business about dragons and stuff. Since we obviously can't get a dragon to cook the nuts to perfection, we are going for the oven instead.

Yield: 1 Cup

Prep Time: 1 hour

Ingredients:

- 1 cup almonds
- ½ tsp salt
- 3 tsp brown sugar
- ½ tsp chili powder
- ½ tsp cayenne powder
- ½ tsp ground cinnamon
- ½ tsp ground cumin
- 1 egg white

Instructions:

1. Preheat oven to 250 degrees F. Prepare a baking sheet lined with parchment paper or grease it with some cooking spray. Set aside.

2. In a bowl mix the spices.

3. Beat the egg white a few times in another bowl. Coat the almonds in it, stirring them with a fork.

4. Transfer the almonds to the bowl of spices to coat completely.

5. Arrange the almonds in the baking sheet, careful not to overlap the nuts with each other.

6. Bake for 50 minutes or until they turn a nice golden brown.

Golden Snitch Cake Bites

The golden snitch signifies victory for our beloved wizard hero. The best way to hail its importance is creating a snack inspired by its existence. That's what this cake bites are all about. It is made with instant cake mix, prepared frosting, edible gold sprinkles, and white fondant for the pretty wings.

Yield: 20 cake bites

Prep Time: 40 Minutes

Ingredients:

- 1 pack Cake mix, prepared according to package directions but baked in lollipop-like molds
- 1 tub frosting
- Yellow candy melts

- Edible gold sprinkles
- White fondant icing

Instructions:

1. Coat cake pops in yellow candy melts, then, coat in golden sprinkles.

2. Cut out wings from white fondant icing. Insert onto small slits on both sides of the cake bites.

3. For the lollie effect, and for that impression that the golden snitch is fluttering, place them onto lollipop sticks.

Canary Cream Sandwich

Canary creams are basically just custard creams that will supposedly turn you into becoming a canary. That is, if magic is involved in the recipe. Don't worry though, as much as this delightful treat can provide a magical effect into your taste buds, it is not magical in the literal sense of the word.

Yield: 8-10 servings

Prep Time: 55 Minutes

Ingredients:

- ¼ cup unsalted butter, softened
- ¼ cup caster sugar
- 1/2 cup flour
- 3 Tbsp. corn flour
- 3 Tbsp. custard powder
- For the filling:
- ¾ cup icing sugar
- 4 Tbsp. butter
- 2 Tbsp. custard powder
- 3 tsp full-cream milk

Instructions:

1. In a mixer, beat together butter and caster sugar until light and fluffy.

2. In a bowl, combine flour, corn flour, and custard powder. Sift the dry ingredients before adding on the butter-sugar mixture. Beat until smooth.

3. Place the dough in a plastic container, chilling in the refrigerator for 20 minutes.

4. Preheat oven to 325 degrees F.

5. Roll prepared dough in a lightly floured surface. Cut 3-4mm thick biscuit and arrange them in a lined baking sheet.

6. Place the baking cookie sheet in the fridge for another 10 minutes before baking.

7. Bake for 10-12 minutes, until the biscuits turn light golden. Place in a wire rack to cool.

8. Meanwhile, mix all the ingredients for the filling until smooth. Transfer into a piping bag and pipe the canary creams filling, placing another biscuit on top to sandwich the filling.

Golden Butterbeer Cupcakes

With all the madness about the heavenly butterbeer drink, we decided to make a cupcake recipe that features its flavors. This may not be as soothing as the real deal, but it is a perfect comfort food that will lift your spirits on bad days and help make celebrating the good days more enjoyable. Just like the drinks version, these Butterbeer cupcakes are made delightful by butterscotch in ganache and buttercream form. Sounds interesting? You bet.

Yield: 18 cupcakes

Prep Time: 45 Minutes

Ingredients:

- 2 cups flour

- 1 ½ tsp baking powder
- ½ tsp baking soda
- Salt
- 1 cup brown sugar
- ½ cup unsalted butter, softened
- 3 eggs
- 2 tsp vanilla extract
- ½ cup buttermilk
- ½ cup cream soda
- ½ cup butterscotch ganache
- 1 cup buttercream

Instructions:

1. Preheat oven to 350 degrees F. Prepare cupcake tins lined with baking cups.

2. Combine flour, baking soda, baking powder, and salt in a bowl. Set aside.

3. Beat butter and brown sugar in a mixer until fluffy and light. Gradually add eggs, one at a time, then vanilla extract.

4. Gradually fold in flour mixture, buttermilk, and cream soda onto butter mixture, careful not to overbeat.

5. Fill cupcake molds ¾ halfway full and bake for 15 minutes or until a toothpick has come out clean. Cool completely.

6. Frost butter beer cupcakes with butterscotch buttercream, then, pour ganache on top.

Broomsticks Treat

Broomsticks play a very significant part in the Harry Potter series not only because our beloved hero is a skilled Quidditch player, a very good one at that. As a potential crowd-drawer in a Harry Potter inspired party, make these broomsticks from pretzel and cheese and you will surely get two thumbs up. This is easy to make, not to mention really cute. A plate would definitely make a nice centerpiece for your Potter feast.

Yield: 10-12 servings

Prep Time: 10 Minutes

Ingredients:

- 1 oz. mozzarella cheese sticks, cut into thirds
- 2 cups pretzel sticks
- Onion chives

Instructions:

1. Create the bottom part of the broomstick from a third of the cheese stick. This is the slightly tedious part since you have to make very little cuts from the small stick but once you get past this stage, it will all be easy.

2. Poke a pretzel stick onto the top part of the cheese.

3. Tie an onion chive around the neck for decorative purposes. Serve.

Wolfsbane Potion

Harry Potter is popular among kids and adults alike. If you are putting together an adult party and you decided to adapt a magical theme, serving cocktails with some Harry Potter flavors is a welcome change. This potion, originally used so Professor Lupin can live through full moons, is one great example. It is succulent and tasty, perfect for any parties.

Yield: 1 Serving

Prep Time: 10 Minutes

Ingredients:

- 1.5 oz. Scotch Whiskey
- 1.5 oz. Fernet-Branca
- Cola

Instructions:

1. Mix whiskey and Fernet-Branca with ice in a shaker until chilled.

2. Transfer into a rocks glass. Top with cola.

Conclusion

Thanks to our awesome kitchen skills, we can help you live the fantasy of recreating Potter world. Enjoy serving your friends and family with the very best drinks, snacks, and whatnots that will allow them to experience the magic altogether.

The recipes we featured on this cookbook are best for hosting ultra exciting and remarkable parties, Harry Potter inspired, of course. They are also great to make everyday 'muggle' meals extra special. Feel free to experience what it's like to be any of your favorite characters in the book – Hermione Granger, Ron Weasley, Hagrid, or even Neville Longbottom!

We are here to prove that you don't really need to have a wand from Ollivander's to cook a fancy feast!

Happy cooking!

Made in the USA
Lexington, KY
27 November 2018